Pathways to Prosperity

Harnessing the Power of Mindset, Attitude and Action

Tom Ray

Copyright © 2023 Tom Ray

All rights reserved. No part of this publication may be reproduced, distributed, or transmitted in any form or by any means without the prior written permission of the author.

ISBN: 979-8-218-95971-5

Dedication

This book is respectfully dedicated to the extraordinary individuals whose wisdom, kindness, and modesty have left a lasting impression on the world. It is a tribute to those who exemplify the highest standards of knowledge and conduct, and who inspire us all to aim for greatness.

To the enlightened and scholarly minds who have lit our paths with their wisdom and insights, I extend my deepest appreciation. Your intellectual strength and commitment to continuous learning have set a brilliant example for us all.

I dedicate this book to my respected mentors and educators, whose guidance and instruction have shaped my intellectual journey. Your patient teaching, unwavering support, and gentle redirection have shaped me into the person I am today. I am eternally grateful for your profound influence.

To my esteemed colleagues and fellow travelers on this intellectual journey, thank you for the thought-provoking discussions, the lively debates, and the companionship that have enriched my understanding and broadened my perspectives. Your intelligence and fellowship have ignited my desire to explore the limits of knowledge.

I dedicate this book to my beloved family, whose steadfast support and unconditional love have been my stronghold throughout this intellectual endeavor. Your faith in me and your encouragement have driven me forward, even in the face of adversity. I am fortunate to have you by my side.

To the readers of this book, I dedicate these words to you, in the knowledge that you, too, are explorers of knowledge and advocates of intellectual growth. May this book serve as a lighthouse, guiding you to new territories of understanding and inspiring you to reach ever greater heights in your pursuit of wisdom.

Lastly, I dedicate this book to future thinkers, those who will take up the torch of knowledge and continue the noble quest for truth. May you carry it with dignity and honor, pushing the boundaries of human understanding and contributing to the betterment of society.

With profound humility and respect, I offer this dedication to you, dear reader, knowing that it is through your engagement and discernment that the true impact of this work will be felt.

With the utmost humility and gratitude.

Acknowledgment

Creating a book is a collective endeavor, and I am profoundly thankful to all those who have contributed to the manifestation of this work. Their support, guidance, and encouragement have been pivotal in bringing this book into existence.

First and foremost, I wish to express my deepest gratitude to my family for their unwavering love and faith in me. Thank you for being my pillar of strength, providing me with the freedom and motivation to follow my passion for writing and personal growth.

I extend my thanks to my friends and colleagues who have provided their invaluable perspectives, feedback, and support throughout the process of writing this book. Your enthusiasm and constructive input have been crucial in refining the ideas and concepts presented within these pages.

I wish to express my sincere appreciation to my mentors and educators, whose wisdom and guidance have illuminated my path. Your knowledge and expertise have been a source of inspiration and have significantly influenced the ideas presented in this book.

I am indebted to the numerous authors, researchers, and thought leaders whose work has laid the groundwork for the concepts discussed in this book. Your commitment to knowledge and personal growth has cleared the path for others to embark on their own transformative journeys.

I would like to extend my gratitude to the publishing team for their diligent work and dedication to bringing this book to completion. Your professionalism, expertise, and meticulous attention to detail have been instrumental in transforming this manuscript into a refined piece of literature.

Lastly, I want to express my deepest gratitude to you, the readers. Thank you for joining me on this journey, for investing your time and energy in exploring the ideas and strategies presented in this book. It is my earnest hope that the insights shared within these pages will empower you to unlock your potential and achieve remarkable success in all facets of your life.

To all those mentioned above and to anyone else who has contributed to this book in any way, please accept my heartfelt thanks. Your support has been invaluable, and I am honored to have you by my side on this incredible journey.

With profound gratitude,

Tom-Ray

About the Author

Tom-Ray Molokwu is renowned for his insightful contributions to unlocking human potential and promoting personal growth. With a lifelong commitment to empowering individuals to discover their inner strength and achieve remarkable success, Tom-Ray has carved a niche for himself as a respected authority in the field of personal development.

Residing in Florida, Tom-Ray brings a rich reservoir of knowledge and a diverse range of expertise to his work. He has pursued academic and professional development across various institutions, thereby broadening his understanding of human behavior and personal growth. Tom-Ray's academic credentials and certifications span a wide array of disciplines, enabling him to provide unique perspectives and insights into the intricacies of the human mind and the pursuit of objectives.

Through his extensive experience as a digital facilitator and his relentless pursuit of personal growth, Tom-Ray has gained a deep understanding of the challenges and opportunities individuals encounter in their personal and professional lives. He has refined his expertise in guiding individuals towards personal transformation and the realization of their aspirations.

In his latest book, "Pathways to Prosperity: A 21-Step Journey to Personal Success and Fulfillment,"

Tom-Ray shares his profound insights into the transformative power of embracing a growth mindset. Drawing from his vast knowledge and experience, he offers practical, actionable advice that readers can implement to unlock their full potential and lead more rewarding and successful lives.

Tom-Ray's work is driven by a genuine passion for the betterment of others and their emotional well-being. He staunchly believes in the significance of emotional agility and its role in achieving personal and professional success. Through his book, he aims to equip readers with the tools and strategies to navigate their emotional terrain, transform their reactions into mindful responses, and achieve their goals.

With his deep understanding of the human psyche and his unwavering commitment to personal growth, Tom-Ray Molokwu has become a beacon of inspiration for individuals seeking to unlock their true potential. His wisdom, experience, and dedication to empowering others radiate brightly through the pages of this transformative book.

Preface: Setting Sail on the Voyage of Success

Welcome to this extraordinary book designed to spark the embers of success within you. It is a compass that will empower you to set sail on a transformative voyage of self-mastery and success. Within the pages of this book, you will uncover a treasure trove of knowledge, insights, and practical guide that would help you to unlock your full potential in navigating the intricate journey to achievement.

Success, though an elusive endeavour to the uninformed, is a unique gem to the beholder. It encompasses not only the attainment of objectives and accomplishments but also the pursuit of personal growth, fulfillment, and the realization of one's authentic purpose. This book, therefore, aims to unravel the intricate strands of success, assisting you in navigating its complexities and releasing the transformative power that resides within you.

As you turn each page, you will embark on a journey of self-discovery, guided by the wisdom and experiences encapsulated within these chapters. From the fundamental principles that anchor success to the strategies that foster resilience and leadership, you will be armed with the tools necessary to surmount challenges and carve your own pathways to greatness.

Throughout this book, you will encounter diverse arrays of topics, each offering unique insights into the multifaceted nature of success. From the power of self-belief and the wonders of effective goal-setting to the profound influence of emotional intelligence and mindfulness, you will unearth the key combinations that mould a life of success.

You will venture into the domains of creativity and innovation, exploring the potency of ideas and the bravery to chase them. You will master the art of effective communication, enabling you to forge impactful connections and collaboration with others towards shared goals. You will navigate the delicate equilibrium of work and personal life, discovering therefrom the tactics to achieve harmony to flourish in all facets of your existence.

This book, therefore, is more than a mere compilation of concepts and strategies. It is further an invitation to embark on a personal journey of self-discovery that would challenge established notions. In the end, you would be able to define success from a personalized rather than jaundiced view. It offers you the opportunity to embrace growth, resilience, and adaptability as success more often than not is birthed from the crucible of daring and the readiness to embrace meaningful change.

As you immerse yourself in these pages, I encourage you to reflect upon your own aspirations, dreams, and objectives. Let the wisdom contained within this book serve as a catalyst for action, propelling you forward on your own unique path towards success. Embrace the power of self-belief, determination, and continuous learning, for these qualities will light your way.

Remember, the voyage towards success is not a solitary endeavor. It is a collective symphony, composed of the experiences, guidance, and support of others. Seek out mentors, coaches, and like-minded individuals who can inspire, challenge, and uplift you along the way. Cultivate a network of support and collaboration, for success thrives in the fertile soil of shared aspirations.

As you set sail on this transformative voyage, I commend you for your dedication, curiosity, and commitment to personal growth. Your decision to embark on this voyage towards success is a testament to your unwavering belief in your potential and your readiness to take the necessary steps to shape a remarkable future.

So, follow me through the pages of this book to explore the adventure that awaits you. In the end, you will learn how to embrace the challenges that lie ahead on your road to success by discovering how to use the reservoirs of your untapped potential.

May this book empower you to reach new horizons, cultivate a life of purpose and fulfillment, and inspire you to leave an indelible mark on the world. Your journey begins now.

Table of Contents

Introduction: Embarking on the Pathways to Prosperity 16

Chapter 1: The Power of Thought 19

Chapter 2: The Rich Mindset 23

Chapter 3: Embracing Change 27

Chapter 4: The Speed of Thought 30

Chapter 5: Cultivating a Positive Attitude 33

Chapter 6: The Power of Goals 36

Chapter 7: The Art of Saving 39

Chapter 8: The Power of Persistence 42

Chapter 9: The Value of Time 45

Chapter 10: The Strength of Relationships 48

Chapter 11: The Power of Knowledge 51

Chapter 12: The Essence of Self-Belief 54

Chapter 13: The Journey of Self-Improvement 57

Chapter 14: The Impact of Positivity 60

Chapter 15: The Influence of Adaptability 63

Chapter 16: The Art of Mindfulness 66

Chapter 17: The Power of Perseverance 69

Chapter 18: The Value of Empathy 72

Chapter 19: The Strength of Humility 75

Chapter 20: The Essence of Communication 78

Chapter 21: The Journey of Lifelong Learning 81

Epilogue: The Symphony of Success 84

REFERENCES 87

"Success is not the key to happiness. Happiness is the key to success. If you love what you are doing, you will be successful."
- *Albert Schweitzer*

Introduction: Embarking on the Pathways to Prosperity

In the vast expanse of human endeavor, there lies a common thread that weaves through every story of triumph, every tale of achievement. It is the relentless pursuit of success, the unyielding desire to progress, and the indomitable spirit that propels us forward in spite of all odds. Yet, the journey to success is not a straight path, but a winding road filled with twists and turns, peaks and valleys, moments of exhilaration, and periods of despair. It is a journey that demands resilience, adaptability, and a mindset geared towards growth and prosperity.

"Pathways to Prosperity: Harnessing the Power of Mindset, Attitude, and Action" is not just a book; it is a compass guiding you through the labyrinth of life towards your personal and professional goals. It is a beacon illuminating the principles that underpin success and progress, principles distilled from the wisdom of some of the most insightful books ever written on these subjects.

Drawing inspiration from the timeless wisdom of Napoleon Hill's "Think and Grow Rich," we delve into the transformative power of thought, the ability to shape our reality through the sheer force of our minds. From the pages of "The Richest Man in Babylon," we glean the secrets of wealth accumulation, the art of saving, and the importance of investing. "Who Moved My Cheese?" lends us the understanding of change and the necessity of adaptability in a world that is in a constant state of flux. "Thinking, Fast and Slow" offers us a deep insight into the intricacies of our thought processes, shedding light on how we make decisions and how our habits shape our lives. And from "Success Through a Positive Mental Attitude," we learn the pivotal role optimism and positivity play in paving the way to success.

This book is not a shortcut to success, for no such shortcut exists. Instead, it is a roadmap that charts the course of success through the terrain of personal growth and professional achievement. Success is a journey that requires persistence, resilience, and a willingness to learn and adapt. It is a journey that demands a positive attitude, a rich mindset, and the courage to embrace change.

This book is designed to take you on a transformative journey to the art of making success of yourself. A journey that will challenge your preconceived notions, stretch your boundaries, and equip you with the necessary tools to navigate the path to success. It is a journey that will not only change the way you view success but also the way you view yourself and the world around you.

Are you ready to embark on this pathway to prosperity? Are you prepared to harness the power of mindset, attitude, and action? If so, let us begin this journey together. Let us explore the principles that underpin success and progress, and through it unlock the potential that lies within each one of us. Welcome to "Pathways to Prosperity."

"As a man thinketh in his heart, so is he."
- *James Allen*

Chapter 1: The Power of Thought

In the grand tapestry of life, our thoughts serve as the threads that weave together the fabric of our reality. They are the drivers of our actions, the sculptors of our attitudes, and the engineers of our destiny. They are the silent whispers that guide our decisions, shape our perceptions, and ultimately determine the course of our lives. This is the profound power of thought, a power that is often underestimated, yet holds the key to unlocking our potential and propelling us towards success.

The concept of the power of thought is not a new one. Philosophers, scientists, and thought leaders have long recognized and explored its influence. However, it was Napoleon Hill's seminal work "Think and Grow Rich," that truly popularized this concept and brought it to the limelight. Hill understood that our thoughts are not mere mental images but potent forces capable of manifesting our deepest desires into reality. This chapter, inspired by Hill's wisdom, delves into the transformative power of thought and its pivotal role in our journey towards success and progress.

Our thoughts, much like a seed, hold within them the potential for growth. A single thought, when nurtured with attention and intention, can blossom into an idea, an action, a habit, and ultimately, a reality. Consider for a moment the achievements of great inventors, scientists, and entrepreneurs. Each of their accomplishments began as a simple thought, a spark of imagination that ignited a flame of innovation and led to groundbreaking discoveries and creations. This is the power of thought in action.

However, the power of thought is not exclusive to the realms of innovation and creation. It extends into every facet of our lives, influencing our attitudes, our behaviors, and our responses to the world around us. Our thoughts shape our perceptions, coloring our view of ourselves and others. They dictate our reactions to life's challenges and opportunities, determining whether we rise to the occasion or succumb to adversity. In essence, our thoughts lay the foundation for our reality, making us the architects of our own lives.

Yet, harnessing the power of thought is not a passive process. It requires conscious effort, deliberate intention, and unwavering focus. It demands that we become active participants in the narrative of our lives, choosing our thoughts wisely and directing them towards our goals. It calls for a shift from a mindset of scarcity, fear, and doubt to one of abundance, courage, and confidence. This shift, while challenging, is the first step towards leveraging the power of thought to propel us towards success.

One effective strategy for harnessing the power of thought is the practice of positive affirmations. Affirmations are positive statements that are repeated with conviction and belief, aimed at reprogramming our subconscious mind and aligning our thoughts with our desires. They serve as a powerful tool for cultivating a positive mindset, boosting self-confidence, and fostering a sense of self-belief. By consistently practicing positive affirmations, we can steer our thoughts towards our goals, thereby setting the stage for their manifestation.

Another strategy is through visualization, a technique that involves creating a mental image of our desired outcome. Visualization works on the premise that our mind cannot distinguish between a vividly imagined experience and a real one. By visualizing our goals as already achieved, we align our thoughts with our desires, thereby attracting the resources, opportunities, and circumstances necessary for their realization.

However, the power of thought is not a magic wand that instantly transforms our desires into reality. It is a tool, a catalyst that, when coupled with action, can bring about remarkable results. Our thoughts, no matter how powerful, must be backed by action to manifest into reality. It is the successful marriage of thought and action that forms the cornerstone of success and progress.

In conclusion, the power of thought is a formidable force that holds the key to our potential pathway to success. By consciously harnessing this power through directing our thoughts towards our goals and backing such thoughts with decisive action, we can shape our reality and chart our course towards success. As we journey through the chapters of this book, let us keep in mind the profound wisdom of Napoleon Hill, "Whatever the mind can conceive and believe, it can achieve." This is the power of thought, the first step on our pathways to prosperity.

> *"Wealth is not about having a lot of money; it's about having a lot of options."*
> - Chris Rock

Chapter 2: The Rich Mindset

In the grand scheme of success and prosperity, mindset stands as a towering pillar, a powerful determinant that shapes our actions, influences our decisions, and ultimately, charts our path towards wealth and abundance. It is the lens through which we view the world, the filter that colors our perceptions, and the compass that guides our journey. This chapter, inspired by the timeless wisdom encapsulated in "The Richest Man in Babylon," delves into the concept of the rich mindset and its pivotal role in our quest for financial success.

The rich mindset is not merely about the accumulation of wealth but rather a holistic approach to life that encompasses a set of beliefs, attitudes, and habits that foster financial success and personal growth. It is about recognizing opportunities, taking calculated risks, and making informed decisions. It is about cultivating resilience, embracing learning, and persisting in the face of adversity to success. Above all, it is about understanding the value of money, not as an end in itself, but as a tool for creating opportunities, achieving goals, and enhancing the quality of life.

At the heart of the rich mindset is the principle of financial literacy. It is the understanding of how money works, the knowledge of investment, savings, and financial management. It is about making your money work for you, rather than you working for your money. This principle, as highlighted in "The Richest Man in Babylon," is the cornerstone of wealth accumulation. By gaining financial literacy, we equip ourselves with the tools necessary to navigate the financial landscape, make informed decisions, and ultimately, build and sustain wealth.

Another key aspect of the rich mindset is the habit of saving. It is the practice of setting aside a portion of our income, not just for rainy days, but for investment and wealth creation. The habit of saving, as simple as it may seem, is a powerful tool for wealth accumulation. It fosters financial discipline, encourages prudent spending, and provides a safety net for unforeseen circumstances. More importantly, it provides the capital necessary for investment, the true engine of wealth creation.

Furthermore, the rich mindset goes beyond financial literacy and saving. It extends into the realm of mindset and attitude. It is about cultivating a positive attitude towards money, viewing it not as a source of stress or anxiety, but as a tool for achieving goals and realizing dreams. It is about embracing the abundance mindset, the belief that there is enough for everyone, and that success does not come at the expense of others. This shift in attitude, while subtle, can have a profound impact on our financial success.

The rich mindset also emphasizes the importance of continuous learning and personal growth. It recognizes that financial success is not a destination, but a journey that requires constant learning, adaptation, and growth. It values knowledge and wisdom, understanding that they are the true wealth that no one can take away. By embracing learning and personal growth, we not only enhance our financial skills but also develop the resilience, adaptability, and creativity necessary for financial success.

The rich mindset however is not just about personal wealth, it also recognizes the importance of giving back. The need to use our wealth to make a positive impact on the world. It understands that true wealth is not measured by the amount of money we have, but by the value we add to the world. By giving back, we not only enrich our lives but also contribute to the betterment of the society.

In conclusion, the rich mindset is a holistic approach to financial success and personal growth. It is a mindset that values financial literacy, cultivates the habit of saving, embraces a positive attitude towards money, values continuous learning, and recognizes the importance of giving back. As we journey through the chapters of this book, let us remember the wisdom of George S. Clason, "Wealth, like a tree, grows from a tiny seed. The first copper you save is the seed from which your tree of wealth shall grow." This is the rich mindset, the second step on our pathways to prosperity.

"Change is the only constant in life."
- *Heraclitus*

Chapter 3: Embracing Change

In the grand symphony of life, change is the only constant. It is the unyielding rhythm that underscores our existence. It is an inevitable force, a dynamic current that propels us forward, reshaping our lives, our perspectives, and our realities. Yet, despite its omnipresence, change is often met with resistance, apprehension, and fear. This chapter, inspired by the wisdom encapsulated in "Who Moved My Cheese?", explores the concept of change and its pivotal role in our progressive success journey.

Change, in its essence, is a transformative process, a shift from one state to another. It can be as subtle as the changing seasons or as dramatic as a career shift, personal as a change in mindset or universal as the invention of a new technology. Regardless of its form or magnitude, change carries with it the potential for growth, innovation, and progress. It is the catalyst that sparks creativity, the stimulus that drives evolution, and the steppingstone that paves the way towards success.

Yet, despite its perceived transformative potential, change is often met with resistance. We cling to the familiar, seeking comfort in the known and predictable. We fear the uncertainty change brings perhaps because of fear of the unknown and the unforeseen. This resistance, while natural, can hinder our growth, limit our potential, and impede our path towards success. It is here that the wisdom of "Who Moved My Cheese?" comes into play, offering valuable insights into why we should embrace change and leverage it for personal and professional growth.

At the heart of embracing change is the ability to let go, to release our grip on the familiar and open ourselves to new possibilities. It is about recognizing that change is not an enemy to be feared, but a friend to be welcomed. It is about understanding that our comfort zone, while safe and predictable, is not a place of growth. By letting go of our resistance, we open the door to new opportunities, new experiences, and new avenues for success.

Another key aspect of embracing change is adaptability, the ability to adjust and thrive in changing circumstances. It is about being flexible, resilient, and open-minded, ready to learn, unlearn, and relearn. It is about being proactive, anticipating change, and preparing for it. By cultivating adaptability, we not only equip ourselves to navigate the winds of change but also to harness them for our benefit.

Yet, embracing change is not just about letting go and adapting. It is also about taking risks, stepping into the unknown, and daring to venture beyond the familiar. It is about viewing change not as a threat, but as an opportunity for growth and innovation. It is about seizing the moment, taking the leap, and daring to explore the uncharted territories of our potential.

However, embracing change does not mean we should recklessly jump into every new opportunity that comes our way. Embracing change requires discernment, the ability to distinguish between changes that align with our goals and values and those that do not. It requires wisdom, the ability to learn from our experiences and use them as a guide in navigating the changing landscape of our lives.

In conclusion, embracing change is a crucial step in our journey towards success and progress. It is about letting go of our resistance, cultivating adaptability, taking calculated risks, and exercising discernment. As we journey through the chapters of this book, let us remember the wisdom of Dr. Spencer Johnson, "What would you do if you weren't afraid?" This is the power of embracing change, the third step on our pathways to prosperity.

"Genius is the ability to put into effect what is in your mind."
- F. Scott Fitzgerald

Chapter 4: The Speed of Thought

In the intricate dance of life, our thoughts serve as the rhythm, guiding our steps, shaping our movements, and ultimately, choreographing our performance. They are the silent whispers that influence our decisions, mold our behaviors, and steer our journey. This chapter, inspired by the insights from "Thinking, Fast and Slow," delves into the dual systems of thought and their profound impact on our path towards success and progress.

Our mind, much like a skilled conductor, orchestrates two distinct systems of thought, each playing a unique role in our cognitive symphony. The first, often referred to as System 1, operates automatically and quickly, with little or no effort and no sense of voluntary control. It is the intuitive, instinctive part of our mind that jumps to conclusions, makes snap judgments, and responds to situations based on gut feelings. The second, known as System 2, is deliberate and slower, involving mental activities that require effort, concentration, and a conscious choice. It is the analytical, logical part of our mind that deliberates, analyzes, and makes calculated decisions.

At first glance, these two systems may seem at odds, each operating at a different pace and with a different approach. However, they are not adversaries but allies, each playing a crucial role in our cognitive process. System 1, with its speed and instinct, enables us to react quickly to situations, making it invaluable in times of danger or urgency. System 2, with its deliberation and analysis, allows us to make informed decisions, making it essential for complex problem-solving and strategic planning.

Yet, while both systems are integral to our cognitive process, their interplay can sometimes lead to biases and errors in judgment. System 1, with its reliance on intuition and instinct, can often jump to conclusions, leading to biases and stereotypes. System 2, despite its analytical prowess, can be lazy, often defaulting to the easier path and relying on System 1. Recognizing these tendencies and understanding their implications is key to harnessing the power of our thoughts and steering our path towards success.

One effective strategy for managing the interplay between the two systems is mindfulness-the practice of being present and aware of our thoughts and actions. By cultivating mindfulness, we can observe our thought process, recognize when System 1 is hastily jumping to conclusions, and therefore engage System 2 to ensure a more balanced and informed decision.

Another strategy is critical thinking-the practice of actively analyzing, evaluating, and synthesizing information. By honing our critical thinking skills, we can engage System 2 more effectively, ensuring that our decisions are not just quick, but also well-informed and well-reasoned.

However, managing the interplay between the two systems is not just about engaging System 2 more effectively. It is also about recognizing the value of System 1, appreciating its speed and instinct, and learning to trust our intuition. It is about finding a balance between the two systems, allowing them to work in harmony rather than in conflict.

In conclusion, the speed of thought, the interplay between the fast, intuitive System 1 and the slow, analytical System 2, plays a crucial role in our journey towards success and progress. By understanding these systems, recognizing their strengths and weaknesses, and learning to manage their interplay, we can harness the power of our thoughts and steer our path towards success. As we journey through the chapters of this book, let us remember the wisdom of Daniel Kahneman, "Your mind will answer most questions if you learn to relax and wait for the answer." This is the speed of thought, the fourth step on our pathways to prosperity.

"Your attitude, not your aptitude, will determine your altitude."
- *Zig Ziglar*

Chapter 5: Cultivating a Positive Attitude

In the vibrant canvas of life, our attitude serves as the palette, coloring our experiences, shaping our perceptions, and ultimately, painting our reality. It is the lens through which we view the world. The filter that influences our reactions, and the compass that guides our journey. This chapter, inspired by the wisdom contained in "Success Through a Positive Mental Attitude," explores the concept of a positive attitude and its pivotal role in our quest for success and progress.

A positive attitude is not merely about wearing a smile or maintaining an outward facade of happiness. It is a deep-seated belief in the positive aspects of life, a conviction in the power of positivity, and a commitment to approach life with optimism and hope. It is about seeing the glass as half full, recognizing opportunities in challenges, and finding silver linings in the darkest of clouds. Above all, it is about cultivating a mindset of abundance, resilience, and gratitude, a mindset that fosters success and progress.

At the heart of a positive attitude is the principle of positivity, the practice of focusing on the positive aspects of life. It is about appreciating the good, celebrating achievements, and acknowledging progress, no matter how small. It is about replacing negative thoughts with positive ones, transforming challenges into opportunities, and setbacks into steppingstones. By cultivating positivity, we not only enhance our mood and energy but also boost our motivation and productivity, thereby propelling us towards success.

Another key aspect of a positive attitude is resilience, the ability to bounce back from adversity, to weather the storms of life, and to emerge stronger and wiser. It is about embracing challenges, learning from failures, and persisting in the face of obstacles. It is about viewing setbacks not as roadblocks, but as detours leading to better paths. By fostering resilience, we not only equip ourselves to handle adversity but also to grow and thrive amidst challenges.

Yet, a positive attitude extends beyond positivity and resilience. It also encompasses gratitude, the practice of acknowledging and appreciating the good in our lives. It is about expressing thanks for our blessings, recognizing the contributions of others, and appreciating the beauty in our world. By practicing gratitude, we not only enhance our happiness and wellbeing but also foster a positive outlook, thereby attracting more positivity into our lives.

Cultivating a positive attitude however, is not about ignoring the negative aspects of life or pretending that everything is perfect. It is about acknowledging the negative, but choosing to focus on the positive. It is about facing challenges, but believing in our ability to overcome them. It is about experiencing setbacks, but never losing sight of our goals. It is this balance between realism and optimism that forms the essence of a positive attitude.

In conclusion, cultivating a positive attitude is a crucial step in our journey towards success and progress. It is about fostering positivity, building resilience, practicing gratitude, and maintaining a balance between realism and optimism. As we journey through the chapters of this book, let us remember the wisdom of Napoleon Hill and W. Clement Stone, "Every adversity, every failure, every heartache carries with it the seed of an equal or greater benefit." This is the power of a positive attitude, the fifth step on our pathways to prosperity.

"A goal properly set is halfway reached."
- *Abraham Lincoln*

Chapter 6: The Power of Goals

In the grand narrative of success and progress, goals serve as the plot points, the milestones that guide our journey, shape our actions, and ultimately, define our story. They are the beacons that illuminate our path, the compass that directs our efforts, and the yardstick that measures our progress. This chapter explores the concept of goal-setting and its pivotal role in our quest for success and progress.

Goals, in their essence, are the destinations we aspire to reach. The dreams we strive to realize, and the visions we endeavor to bring to life. They are the manifestations of our desires, ambitions, and aspirations, crystallized into tangible targets. They provide us with direction, foster motivation, and instill a sense of purpose that propels us forward.

At the heart of goal-setting is the principle of clarity. It is about defining our goals with precision and specificity, transforming vague aspirations into clear, actionable targets. It is about knowing what we want to achieve, why we want to achieve it, and how we plan to achieve it. By establishing clear goals, we create a roadmap for success, a guide that directs our efforts and keeps us on track.

Another key aspect of goal-setting is realism, which is setting goals that are challenging yet achievable, ambitious yet within reach. It is about assessing our capabilities, recognizing our limitations, and setting goals that stretch us without overwhelming us. By setting realistic goals, we not only increase our chances of success but also boost our motivation and self-confidence.

Yet, goal-setting extends beyond clarity and realism. It also encompasses commitment. The unwavering dedication to reach our goals, and the steadfast resolve to see them through. It is about staying on course, persisting in the face of obstacles, and maintaining focus amidst distractions. By committing to our goals, we not only fuel our motivation but also strengthen our resilience, thereby enhancing our chances of success.

Goal-setting however, is not a one-time event, but an ongoing process. It requires regular review and adjustment, taking into account our progress, changes in circumstances, and new insights. It is about being flexible, ready to revise our goals as needed, and willing to adapt our strategies as required. This flexibility, while maintaining our commitment, is key to effective goal-setting.

In conclusion, the power of goals is a formidable force, one that shapes our actions, directs our journey, and propels us towards success. By setting clear and realistic goals, committing to them, and reviewing them regularly, we can harness this power and steer our path towards success. As we journey through the chapters of this book, let us be guided by the wisdom of Antoine de Saint-Exupéry, "A goal without a plan is just a wish." This is the power of goals, the sixth step on our pathways to prosperity.

> *"Do not save what is left after spending; instead, spend what is left after saving."*
> - *Warren Buffett*

Chapter 7: The Art of Saving

In the intricate mosaic of financial success, saving serves as a fundamental piece, a cornerstone that supports our financial structure and ultimately shapes our financial future. It is the practice that safeguards our present, secures our future, and paves the way for wealth accumulation. This chapter, drawing inspiration from the wisdom encapsulated in "The Richest Man in Babylon," explores the art of saving and its pivotal role in our journey towards financial prosperity.

Saving, in its essence, is the act of setting aside a portion of our income for future use. It is a practice that requires discipline, patience, and foresight. A commitment to forgo immediate gratification for long-term benefits. It is about taking control of our financial destiny, building a safety net for unforeseen circumstances, and creating a foundation for wealth accumulation.

At the heart of the art of saving is the principle of 'paying oneself first.' It is about prioritizing our financial future, setting aside a portion of our income for savings before addressing other expenses. This principle, as highlighted in "The Richest Man in Babylon," is the first step towards financial independence. By paying ourselves first, we not only secure our financial future but also cultivate financial discipline, a key attribute for financial success.

Another key aspect of the art of saving is consistency. It is about internalizing the habit of regular saving, regardless of the amount. It is about making saving a non-negotiable part of our financial routine. By saving consistently, we not only accumulate wealth over time but also instill a sense of financial discipline, thereby enhancing our financial management skills.

Yet, the art of saving extends beyond paying oneself first and consistency. It also encompasses prudence, the ability to manage our finances wisely, to differentiate between needs and wants, and to make informed spending decisions. It is about living within our means, avoiding unnecessary debts, and making the most of our income. By practicing prudence, we not only enhance our saving potential but also foster a healthy relationship with money.

However, saving is not an end in itself, but a means to an end. It is the capital that fuels investment, the engine of wealth creation. It is the seed that, when sown wisely, can grow into a tree of wealth. Therefore, while saving is crucial, it is equally important to learn how to invest our savings wisely, to make our money work for us. This balance between saving and investing is key to financial prosperity.

In conclusion, the art of saving is a fundamental step in our journey towards financial success. It is about paying ourselves first, saving consistently, practicing prudence, and investing wisely. As we journey through the chapters of this book, let us remember the wisdom of George S. Clason, "A part of all you earn is yours to keep. It should be not less than a tenth no matter how little you earn. It can be as much more as you can afford." This is the art of saving, the seventh step on our pathways to prosperity.

> *"Success is not final, failure is not fatal: It is the courage to continue that counts."*
> - *Winston Churchill*

Chapter 8: The Power of Persistence

In the grand theater of success and progress, persistence plays a starring role, a compelling performance that shapes our actions, influences our journey, and ultimately, determines our destiny. It is the unwavering commitment to our goals, the relentless pursuit of our dreams, and the steadfast resolve to overcome obstacles. This chapter explores the power of persistence and its pivotal role in our quest for success and progress.

Persistence, in its essence, is the tenacity to keep going. It is the determination to keep trying, and the resilience to keep fighting, despite the odds, setbacks, and failures. It is a testament to our strength, a reflection of our commitment, and a measure of our resilience. It is about standing firm in the face of adversity, holding on to our dreams in the midst of challenges, and marching forward on our path, no matter how rough or winding it may be.

At the heart of persistence is the principle of resilience, the ability to bounce back from setbacks, to rise from failures, and to recover from disappointments. It is about viewing failures not as the end, but as steppingstones to success, as opportunities to learn, grow, and become stronger. By cultivating resilience, we not only equip ourselves to handle adversity but also to thrive amidst challenges, thereby enhancing our chances of success.

Another key aspect of persistence is patience-the ability to wait, to endure, and to keep going, even when progress is slow or results are not immediate. It is about understanding that success is not an overnight phenomenon, but a journey that requires time, effort, and perseverance. By practicing patience, we not only manage our expectations but also maintain our motivation, thereby fueling our persistence.

Yet, persistence extends beyond resilience and patience. It also encompasses adaptability, the ability to adjust our strategies, change our approach, and modify our plans in response to changing circumstances or feedback. It is about being flexible, ready to learn from our experiences, and willing to change our course, if necessary. This adaptability, while maintaining our commitment to our goals, is key to effective persistence.

However, persistence is not about stubbornly clinging to a failing plan or refusing to acknowledge a dead-end. It requires discernment, the ability to recognize when a change of direction is needed, when a goal is no longer viable, or when a strategy is not working. It is about being persistent in our pursuit of success, but flexible in our approach, ready to adapt, or even let go, if necessary.

In conclusion, the power of persistence is a formidable force, one that propels us forward, fuels our journey, and paves our path towards success. By cultivating resilience, practicing patience, embracing adaptability, and exercising discernment, we can harness this power and steer our course towards success. As we journey through the chapters of this book, let us recall the wisdom of Calvin Coolidge, "Nothing in this world can take the place of persistence. Talent will not; nothing is more common than unsuccessful men with talent. Genius will not; unrewarded genius is almost a proverb. Education will not; the world is full of educated derelicts. Persistence and determination alone are omnipotent." This is the power of persistence, the eighth step on our pathways to prosperity.

"Lost time is never found again."
- *Benjamin Franklin*

Chapter 9: The Value of Time

In the grand scheme of success and progress, time serves as the canvas. It is the medium upon which our actions, decisions, and experiences are etched. It is the most precious resource we possess, the one commodity that, once spent, can never be regained. This chapter, inspired by the wisdom garnered in "The 7 Habits of Highly Effective People," explores the concept of time management and its pivotal role in our journey towards success and progress.

Time management, in its essence, is the art of organizing and using our time effectively to achieve our goals. It is about prioritizing tasks, setting schedules, and making conscious decisions about what to do and when to do it. It is about maximizing productivity, minimizing stress, and achieving a balance between work and personal life. Above all, it is about recognizing the value of time and using it wisely to create a fulfilling and successful life.

At the heart of time management is the principle of prioritization, the practice of ranking tasks based on their importance and urgency. It is about knowing and prioritizing what is important and can contribute to our goals and values. In essence, paying attention to what is urgent and demands immediate attention. By prioritizing tasks, we ensure that our time and energy are invested in activities that align with our goals, thereby enhancing our productivity and effectiveness.

Another key aspect of time management is planning-the process of mapping out our tasks, setting timelines, and allocating resources. It is about creating a road-map for our daily, weekly, monthly or even yearly activities, providing a clear direction and a sense of control. By planning our time, we not only increase our productivity but also reduce stress, thereby enhancing our overall well-being.

Time management extends beyond prioritization and planning. It also encompasses discipline, the ability to stick to our schedule, resist distractions, and maintain focus. It is about developing a strong work ethic, cultivating self-control, and fostering a sense of responsibility. By exercising discipline, we not only ensure effective execution of our plans but also build a strong foundation for success.

Effective time management, however, is not limited to work and productivity. It also holistic self-management including time for rest, relaxation, and personal growth. It is about striking a balance between work and personal life. This balance, while often challenging to achieve, is crucial for maintaining our physical, mental, and emotional health, thereby enhancing our overall effectiveness and success.

In conclusion, the value of time is a fundamental aspect of success and progress. By mastering the art of time management, by prioritizing tasks, planning our time, exercising discipline, and maintaining a work-life balance, we can harness the power of time and steer our path towards success. As we journey through the chapters of this book, let us remember the wisdom of Stephen R. Covey, "The key is in not spending time, but in investing it." This is the value of time, the ninth step on our pathways to prosperity.

> *"Friendship is born at that moment when one person says to another, 'What! You too? I thought I was the only one.'"*
> - *C.S. Lewis*

Chapter 10: The Strength of Relationships

In the grand tapestry of success and progress, relationships serve as the threads, the connections that bind our experiences, shape our identities, and ultimately, define our lives. They are the bridges that link us to others, the networks that expand our horizons, and the bonds that enrich our lives. This chapter, inspired by the wisdom encapsulated in "How to Win Friends and Influence People," explores the concept of relationships and their pivotal role in our journey towards success and progress.

Relationships, in their essence, are the connections we form with others. They are the bonds we forge through shared experiences an entails mutual respect and genuine affection. They are the channels through which we interact with the world, the mirrors that reflect our humanity, and the catalysts that spark our growth. Relationships indeed are about understanding and being understood, giving and receiving, sharing and caring. Above all, they are about recognizing the inherent value of others and cherishing the richness they bring to our lives.

At the heart of building strong relationships is the principle of empathy-the ability to see things from the lenses or the understanding and feelings of others. It is about stepping into their shoes, seeing the world through their eyes, and connecting with their experiences. By practicing empathy, we not only foster deeper connections but also cultivate a sense of compassion and kindness, thereby enriching our relationships.

Another key aspect of building strong relationships is communication, the exchange of thoughts, ideas, and emotions. It is about expressing ourselves clearly, listening attentively, and responding thoughtfully. It is about fostering open dialogue, encouraging constructive feedback, and promoting mutual understanding. By honing our communication skills, we not only enhance our interactions but also strengthen our relationships.

Yet, building strong relationships extends beyond empathy and communication. It also encompasses respect, the acknowledgment of the worth and dignity of others. It is about valuing their opinions, appreciating their contributions, and honoring their rights. It is about treating others with kindness, fairness, and integrity, thereby fostering a sense of trust and mutual respect.

However, building strong relationships is not a one-way street. It involves reciprocity-the practice of giving and receiving, contributing and benefiting. It is about investing in our relationships, nurturing them with time, effort, and care. It is about being there for others, not just in times of joy and celebration, but also in times of hardship and sorrow.

In conclusion, the strength of relationships is a formidable force that enhances our lives, enriches our experiences, and propels us towards success. By cultivating empathy, honing our communication skills, practicing respect, and fostering reciprocity, we can build strong relationships and harness their power for our success. As we journey through the chapters of this book, let us remember the wisdom of Dale Carnegie, "You can make more friends in two months by becoming interested in other people than you can in two years by trying to get other people interested in you." This is the strength of relationships, the tenth step on our pathways to prosperity.

> *"The only true wisdom is in knowing you know nothing."*
> - Socrates

Chapter 11: The Power of Knowledge

In the grand architecture of success and progress, knowledge serves as the foundation, the bedrock upon which our actions, decisions, and experiences are built. It is the tool that sharpens our minds, the fuel that drives our curiosity, and the compass that guides our exploration. This chapter, drawing inspiration from the wisdom encapsulated in "The Alchemist," explores the concept of knowledge and its pivotal role in our journey towards success and progress.

Knowledge, in its essence, is the understanding and awareness of facts, information, skills, and concepts. It is the product of learning, the fruit of curiosity, and the outcome of exploration. It is about understanding the world around us, mastering our craft, and expanding our horizons. Above all, it is about recognizing the power of learning and committing to the pursuit of knowledge.

At the heart of the power of knowledge is the principle of curiosity, the desire to learn, explore, and understand. It is about asking questions, seeking answers, and challenging assumptions. It is about embracing the unknown, venturing beyond the familiar, and daring to delve into the depths of the unexplored. By cultivating curiosity, we not only fuel our learning but also foster a sense of wonder and fascination, thereby enriching our journey towards knowledge.

Another key aspect of the power of knowledge is learning, the process of acquiring, assimilating, and applying information. It is about reading, observing, experimenting, and reflecting. It is about learning from our experiences, learning from others, and learning from the world around us. By committing to lifelong learning, we not only expand our knowledge but also enhance our adaptability, creativity, and problem-solving skills.

Yet, the power of knowledge extends beyond curiosity and learning. It also encompasses wisdom, the ability to use our knowledge judiciously, to make informed decisions, and to navigate the complexities of life. It is about discerning the truth, understanding the consequences, and choosing the right path. By cultivating wisdom, we not only harness the power of knowledge but also foster a sense of integrity and responsibility.

However, the pursuit of knowledge is not just about acquiring information or mastering skills. It is also about understanding ourselves, our strengths, our weaknesses, our passions, and our purpose. It is about self-discovery, self-awareness, and self-improvement. This introspective aspect of knowledge, while often overlooked, is crucial for personal growth and self-fulfillment.

In conclusion, the power of knowledge is a formidable force, one that shapes our minds, enriches our lives, and propels us towards success. By cultivating curiosity, committing to lifelong learning, fostering wisdom, and pursuing self-knowledge, we can harness this power and steer our path towards success. As we journey through the chapters of this book, let us remember the wisdom of Paulo Coelho, "Everyone seems to have a clear idea of how other people should lead their lives, but none about his or her own." This is the power of knowledge, the eleventh step on our pathways to prosperity.

"Whether you think you can or you think you can't, you're right."
- *Henry Ford*

Chapter 12: The Essence of Self-Belief

In the grand symphony of success and progress, self-belief serves as the melody. The tune that harmonizes our actions, orchestrates our performance, and ultimately, composes our life's song. It is the faith we have in ourselves, the conviction in our abilities, and the confidence in our potential. This chapter, inspired by the wisdom encapsulated in "The Magic of Thinking Big," explores the concept of self-belief and its pivotal role in our journey towards success and progress.

Self-belief, in its essence, is the trust we place in ourselves, the assurance we have in our capabilities, and the confidence we hold in our worth. It is the voice within us that whispers, "You can do it," the inner strength that propels us forward, and the inner light that guides our path. It is about recognizing our potential, acknowledging our worth, and embracing our uniqueness. Above all, it is about believing in our power to shape our destiny and create our success.

At the heart of self-belief is the principle of self-acceptance, that is, the practice of acknowledging and embracing ourselves, with all our strengths and weaknesses, successes and failures, virtues and flaws. It is about celebrating our achievements, learning from our mistakes, and appreciating our uniqueness. By practicing self-acceptance, we not only foster self-belief but also cultivate self-love, thereby enhancing our self-esteem and self-confidence.

Another key aspect of self-belief is self-efficacy, the belief in our ability to accomplish tasks and achieve goals. It is about setting realistic expectations, taking calculated risks, and facing challenges with courage and determination. By fostering self-efficacy, we not only enhance our performance but also boost our motivation and resilience, thereby propelling us towards success.

Yet, self-belief extends beyond self-acceptance and self-efficacy. It also encompasses self-compassion, the practice of treating ourselves with kindness, understanding, and forgiveness. It is about being gentle with ourselves when we make mistakes, being patient with ourselves when we struggle, and being kind to ourselves when we suffer. By practicing self-compassion, we not only heal our wounds but also strengthen our self-belief, thereby fostering a healthy relationship with ourselves.

However, self-belief is not about arrogance or overconfidence. It is not about ignoring our weaknesses or denying our failures. It is about acknowledging our imperfections, learning from our shortcomings, and striving for improvement. It is about being humble in our strengths, resilient in our failures, and persistent in our efforts. This balance between confidence and humility, between self-belief and self-improvement, is key to authentic self-belief.

In conclusion, the essence of self-belief is a powerful force, one that shapes our identity, influences our actions, and propels us towards success. By cultivating self-acceptance, fostering self-efficacy, practicing self-compassion, and maintaining a balance between confidence and humility, we can harness the power of self-belief and steer our path towards success. As we journey through the chapters of this book, let us remember the wisdom of David J. Schwartz, "Believe it can be done. When you believe something can be done, really believe, your mind will find the ways to do it." This is the essence of self-belief, the twelfth step on our pathways to prosperity.

"Be a student of life. Keep learning, keep growing, and keep evolving. The journey of self-improvement is the path to unlocking your true potential."
- *Robin Sharma*

Chapter 13: The Journey of Self-Improvement

In the grand narrative of success and progress, self-improvement serves as a recurring theme, a continuous subplot that weaves through our experiences, shapes our character, and ultimately, enriches our life's story. It is the commitment to personal growth, the pursuit of betterment, and the quest for excellence. This chapter, inspired by the wisdom encapsulated in "Awaken the Giant Within," explores the concept of self-improvement and its pivotal role in our journey towards success and progress.

Self-improvement, in its essence, is the endeavor to enhance our skills, expand our knowledge, and elevate our character. It is the journey of becoming the best version of ourselves, of realizing our potential, and of transcending our limitations. It is about learning and growing, evolving and transforming, aspiring and achieving. Above all, it is about recognizing our capacity for change and harnessing it to create a fulfilling and successful life.

At the heart of self-improvement is the principle of lifelong learning, the commitment to continuous education, exploration, and enlightenment. It is about nurturing our curiosity, expanding our horizons, and deepening our understanding. By embracing lifelong learning, we not only enhance our knowledge and skills but also foster a sense of wonder and fascination, thereby enriching our journey of self-improvement.

Another key aspect of self-improvement is self-reflection, the practice of introspection, contemplation, and self-examination. It is about assessing our actions, analyzing our decisions, and evaluating our progress. It is about gaining insights into our thoughts, emotions, and behaviors, and using these insights to guide our growth and development. By practicing self-reflection, we not only enhance our self-awareness but also foster self-understanding, thereby empowering our self-improvement.

Yet, self-improvement extends beyond lifelong learning and self-reflection. It also encompasses self-discipline, the ability to control our impulses, resist temptations, and maintain focus. It is about setting goals, creating plans, and following through. It is about cultivating good habits, breaking bad ones, and striving for consistency. By exercising self-discipline, we not only enhance our productivity but also strengthen our character, thereby accelerating our self-improvement.

However, self-improvement is not about striving for perfection or comparing ourselves to others. It is about recognizing our uniqueness, appreciating our journey, and celebrating our progress. It is about being patient with ourselves, being kind to ourselves, and being proud of ourselves. This balance between striving for betterment and practicing self-compassion is key to authentic self-improvement.

In conclusion, the journey of self-improvement is a powerful expedition, one that shapes our character, enriches our experiences, and propels us towards success. By embracing lifelong learning, practicing self-reflection, exercising self-discipline, and maintaining a balance between striving and self-compassion, we can embark on this journey and steer our path towards success. As we journey through the chapters of this book, let us remember the wisdom of Tony Robbins, "The only impossible journey is the one you have never begun." This is the journey of self-improvement, the thirteenth step on our pathways to prosperity.

"The greatest weapon against stress and negativity is our ability to choose one positive thought over another."
- William James

Chapter 14: The Impact of Positivity

In the grand panorama of success and progress, positivity serves as the sunlight, the radiant energy that illuminates our path, warms our journey, and ultimately, brightens our life's landscape. It is the optimistic outlook, the hopeful perspective, and the cheerful attitude. This chapter, inspired by the wisdom encapsulated in "The Power of Positive Thinking," explores the concept of positivity and its pivotal role in our journey towards success and progress.

Positivity, in its essence, is the practice of focusing on the good. The habit of seeing the silver lining, and the courage to embrace hope. It is the lens through which we view our experiences, the filter through which we interpret our reality, and the mindset with which we approach our challenges. It is about recognizing the beauty in our journey, appreciating the blessings in our life, and celebrating the goodness in our world. Above all, it is about believing in the power of optimism and harnessing it to create a fulfilling and successful life.

At the heart of positivity is the principle of gratitude, the practice of acknowledging and appreciating the good in our life. It is about counting our blessings, cherishing our joys, and celebrating our achievements. By cultivating gratitude, we not only enhance our positivity but also foster a sense of contentment and happiness, thereby enriching our life's experience.

Another key aspect of positivity is resilience, the ability to bounce back from adversity, to recover from setbacks, and to rise from failures. It is about viewing challenges as opportunities, setbacks as lessons, and failures as steppingstones to success. By fostering resilience, we not only enhance our ability to cope with adversity but also boost our positivity, thereby empowering our journey towards success.

Yet, positivity extends beyond gratitude and resilience. It also encompasses hope, the belief in a better future, the faith in our potential, and the confidence in our journey. It is about dreaming big, aiming high, and believing in our ability to achieve our goals. By embracing hope, we not only fuel our motivation but also strengthen our positivity, thereby propelling us towards success.

However, positivity is not about denying reality or ignoring the existence of problems. It is not about wearing rose-tinted glasses or living in a bubble of delusion. It is about acknowledging the challenges, addressing the issues, and yet choosing to focus on the good, to believe in the possible, and to hope for the best. This balance between realism and optimism, between acknowledging the negative and focusing on the positive, is key to authentic positivity.

In conclusion, the impact of positivity is a powerful force, one that brightens our path, fuels our journey, and propels us towards success. By cultivating gratitude, fostering resilience, embracing hope, and maintaining a balance between realism and optimism, we can harness the power of positivity and steer our path towards success. As we journey through the chapters of this book, let us remember the wisdom of Norman Vincent Peale, "Change your thoughts and you change your world." This is the impact of positivity, the fourteenth step on our pathways to prosperity.

"The measure of intelligence is the ability to change."
- *Albert Einstein*

Chapter 15: The Influence of Adaptability

In the grand journey of success and progress, adaptability serves as the compass: the instrument that guides our navigation, adjusts our course, and ultimately, determines our destination. It is the ability to adjust to change, the capacity to evolve with circumstances, and the flexibility to alter our path. This chapter, inspired by the wisdom encapsulated in "Who Moved My Cheese?" explores the concept of adaptability and its pivotal role in our journey towards success and progress.

Adaptability, in its essence, is the capacity to change or be changed in order to fit or work better in some situation or for some purpose. It is the ability to alter our thoughts, actions, and strategies in response to changing circumstances. It is about being flexible in our approach, open to new ideas, and willing to step out of our comfort zone. Above all, it is about recognizing the inevitability of change and harnessing it to create a fulfilling and successful life.

At the heart of adaptability is the principle of open-mindedness, that is, the willingness to consider new ideas, perspectives, and possibilities. It is about challenging our assumptions, questioning our beliefs, and exploring new paradigms. By cultivating open-mindedness, we not only enhance our adaptability but also foster a sense of curiosity and innovation, thereby enriching our journey towards success.

Another key aspect of adaptability is resilience, the ability to recover from setbacks, adapt to change, and keep going in the face of adversity. It is about viewing challenges as opportunities for growth, setbacks as lessons for improvement, and failures as steppingstones to success. By fostering resilience, we not only enhance our ability to cope with adversity but also boost our adaptability, thereby empowering our journey towards success.

Yet, adaptability extends beyond open-mindedness and resilience. It also encompasses courage, the willingness to take risks, to venture into the unknown, and to embrace change. It is about daring to step out of our comfort zone, to try new things, and to explore new paths. By embracing courage, we not only fuel our adventurous spirit but also strengthen our adaptability, thereby propelling us towards success.

However, adaptability is not about aimlessly drifting with the wind or mindlessly conforming to the crowd. It is about being flexible in our approach, firm in our values, adaptable in our strategies and steadfast in our goals. This balance between flexibility and firmness is key to authentic adaptability.

In conclusion, the influence of adaptability is a powerful force, one that shapes our journey, enriches our experiences, and propels us towards success. By cultivating open-mindedness, fostering resilience, embracing courage, and maintaining a balance between flexibility and firmness, we can harness the power of adaptability and steer our path towards success. As we journey through the chapters of this book, let us remember the wisdom of Spencer Johnson, "What would you do if you weren't afraid?" This is the influence of adaptability, the fifteenth step on our pathways to prosperity.

"The present moment is filled with joy and happiness. If you are attentive, you will see it."
- *Thich Nhat Hanh*

Chapter 16: The Art of Mindfulness

In the grand canvas of success and progress, mindfulness serves as the brushstroke. The delicate touch that adds depth, texture, and ultimately, beauty to our life's masterpiece. It is the practice of being present, the habit of paying attention, and the discipline of living in the moment. This chapter, inspired by the wisdom encapsulated in "The Power of Now," explores the concept of mindfulness and its pivotal role in our journey towards success and progress.

Mindfulness, in its essence, is the practice of focusing our attention on the present moment, of being fully engaged in the here and now. It is about observing our thoughts, feelings, and sensations without judgment, aware of our surroundings without distraction. It is about experiencing life as it unfolds, savoring each moment as it comes, and cherishing each experience as it happens. Above all, it is about recognizing the power of the present and harnessing it to create a fulfilling and successful life.

At the heart of mindfulness is the principle of attention. The practice of focusing our mind, directing our thoughts, and controlling our consciousness. It is about being present in our actions, attentive in our interactions, and alive to our experiences. By cultivating attention, we not only enhance our mindfulness but also foster a sense of clarity and concentration, thereby enriching our journey towards success.

Another key aspect of mindfulness is acceptance, the practice of acknowledging our thoughts, feelings, and sensations without judgment or resistance. It is about accepting our experiences as they are, embracing our emotions as they come, and acknowledging our thoughts as they arise. By fostering acceptance, we not only enhance our emotional well-being but also deepen our mindfulness, thereby empowering our journey towards success.

Yet, mindfulness extends beyond attention and acceptance. It also encompasses gratitude, the practice of appreciating the present, cherishing the now, and celebrating the moment. It is about savoring the beauty of the present, appreciating the blessings of the now, and expressing gratitude for the moment. By embracing gratitude, we not only enrich our experiences but also amplify our mindfulness towards success.

However, mindfulness is not about escaping reality or avoiding responsibilities. It is not about living in a bubble of the present or ignoring the past or future. It is about being fully present in the moment, but also learning from the past and planning for the future. This balance between living in the present and acknowledging the continuum of time is key to authentic mindfulness.

In conclusion, the art of mindfulness is a powerful practice that enriches our experiences, enhances our awareness, and propels us towards success. By cultivating attention, fostering acceptance, embracing gratitude, and maintaining a balance between the present and the continuum of time, we can master the art of mindfulness and steer our path towards success. As we journey through the chapters of this book, let us remember the wisdom of Eckhart Tolle, "Realize deeply that the present moment is all you have. Make the NOW the primary focus of your life." This is the art of mindfulness, the sixteenth step on our pathways to prosperity.

"Perseverance is not a long race; it is many short races one after the other."
- *Walter Elliot*

Chapter 17: The Power of Perseverance

In the grand marathon of success and progress, perseverance serves as the enduring stride, the relentless pace that propels us forward to overcome obstacles, and ultimately carry us across the finish line. It is the steadfast determination, the unwavering commitment, and the unyielding resolve. This chapter, inspired by the wisdom encapsulated in "Grit: The Power of Passion and Perseverance," explores the concept of perseverance and its pivotal role in our journey towards success and progress.

Perseverance, in its essence, is the tenacity to keep going, the grit to keep fighting, and the resilience to keep bouncing back. It is about staying committed to our goals, persisting in the face of adversity, and refusing to give up in the face of failure. It is about embracing challenges, overcoming obstacles, and conquering difficulties. Above all, it is about recognizing the power of persistence and harnessing it to create a fulfilling and successful life.

At the heart of perseverance is the principle of determination, the unwavering commitment to our goals, the relentless pursuit of our dreams, and the steadfast resolve to achieve our aspirations. It is about setting our sights on our goals, focusing our efforts on our objectives, and directing our energy towards our ambitions. By cultivating determination, we not only enhance our perseverance but also foster a sense of purpose and direction, thereby enriching our journey towards success.

Another key aspect of perseverance is resilience, the ability to recover from setbacks, adapt to change, and keep going in the face of adversity. It is about viewing challenges as opportunities for growth, setbacks as lessons for improvement, and failures as steppingstones to success. By fostering resilience, we not only enhance our ability to cope with adversity but also boost our perseverance, hence, empowering our journey towards success.

Perseverance extends beyond determination and resilience. It also encompasses patience, the capacity to tolerate delay, the ability to endure hardship, and the willingness to wait for the fruits of our labor. It is about understanding that success is a journey, progress a process and not an event. By embracing patience, we not only cultivate a sense of peace and contentment but also strengthen our perseverance, thereby propelling us towards success.

It must be stated that perseverance is not about stubbornly clinging to unattainable goals or persisting in futile endeavors. It is about being flexible in our approach, adaptable in our strategies, and open to new possibilities. This balance between persistence and flexibility, between tenacity and adaptability, is key to authentic perseverance.

In conclusion, the power of perseverance is a formidable force, one that shapes our journey, fuels our progress, and propels us towards success. By cultivating determination, fostering resilience, embracing patience, and maintaining a balance between persistence and flexibility, we can harness the power of perseverance and steer our path towards success. As we journey through the chapters of this book, let us remember the wisdom of Angela Duckworth, "Grit is sticking with your future, day in, day out, not just for the week, not just for the month, but for years, and working really hard to make that future a reality." This is the power of perseverance, the seventeenth step on our pathways to prosperity.

"Empathy is about standing in someone else's shoes, feeling with his or her heart, seeing with his or her eyes. Not only is empathy hard to outsource and automate, but it makes the world a better place." - Daniel H. Pink

Chapter 18: The Value of Empathy

In the grand tapestry of success and progress, empathy serves as the delicate yet strong fiber thread that connects us to others, weaves our relationships, and ultimately enriches our life's design. It is the ability to understand and share the feelings of others. The capacity to step into their shoes and the willingness to see the world from their perspective. This chapter, inspired by the wisdom encapsulated in "Emotional Intelligence," explores the concept of empathy and its pivotal role in our journey towards success and progress.

Empathy simply put is the practice of understanding, sharing, and responding to the emotional states of others. It is about perceiving their feelings, comprehending their experiences, and acknowledging their perspectives. It is about connecting with others on a deeper level, building meaningful relationships, and fostering a sense of unity and togetherness. Above all, it is about recognizing the value of emotional connection and harnessing it to create a fulfilling and successful life.

Underpinning the principle of empathy is understanding: the practice of perceiving and comprehending the emotions, experiences, and perspectives of others. It is about listening with an open mind, observing with a keen eye, and responding with a compassionate heart. By cultivating understanding, we not only enhance our empathy but also foster a sense of connection and unity, thereby enriching our journey towards success.

A common thread of empathy is compassion, the feeling of shared suffering and the desire to alleviate it. It is about feeling for others, caring for their well-being, and helping them in their struggles. By showing compassion, we demonstrate our humanity, spice up our emotional well-being and create goodwill even unknowingly for ourselves. Goodwill is a strong currency to our journey towards success.

Yet, empathy extends beyond understanding and compassion. It also encompasses respect, the acknowledgment of the feelings, experiences, and perspectives of others. It is about respecting their emotions, appreciating their experiences, and honoring their perspectives. By embracing respect, we not only cultivate a sense of dignity and worth but also strengthen our empathy, thereby propelling us towards success.

However, empathy is not about losing ourselves in the emotions of others or neglecting our own feelings and needs. It is about balancing our emotional engagement with others with our self-care and self-awareness. This balance between empathy for others and care for self is key to authentic empathy.

In conclusion, the value of empathy is a powerful asset, one that enriches our relationships, enhances our emotional intelligence, and propels us towards success. By cultivating understanding, fostering compassion, embracing respect, and maintaining a balance between empathy for others and care for self, we can harness the value of both empathy and goodwill, and steer our path towards success. As we journey through the chapters of this book, let us remember the wisdom of Daniel Goleman, "Empathy represents the foundation skill for all the social competencies important for work." This is the value of empathy, the eighteenth step on our pathways to prosperity.

"True humility is not thinking less of yourself; it is thinking of yourself less." - C.S. Lewis

Chapter 19: The Strength of Humility

In the grand architecture of success and progress, humility serves as the foundation, the bedrock that supports our growth, stabilizes our journey, and ultimately, underpins our life's structure. It is the modest view of one's importance, the unassuming regard for oneself, and the humble appreciation of our place in the world. This chapter, inspired by the wisdom contained in "Good to Great," explores the concept of humility and its pivotal role in our journey towards success and progress.

Humility, in its essence, is the practice of maintaining a modest view of our own importance. It is about recognizing our strengths without arrogance, acknowledging our weaknesses without self-deprecation, and appreciating our worth without vanity. It is about being grounded in our successes, hopefully futuristic in our failures, and balanced in our self-perception. Above all, it is about recognizing the value of humility and harnessing it to create a fulfilling and successful life.

At the heart of humility is the principle of self-awareness, the practice of understanding our thoughts, feelings, and behaviors. It is about recognizing our strengths, acknowledging our weaknesses, and understanding that our actions have impacts in the lives of others. By cultivating self-awareness, we not only enhance our humility but also foster a sense of authenticity and integrity, thereby enriching our journey towards success.

Another key aspect of humility is respect, the practice of acknowledging and appreciating the value and worth of others. It is about recognizing their strengths, appreciating their contributions, and valuing their perspectives. By fostering respect, we not only enhance our relationships but also deepen our humility, thereby empowering our journey towards success.

Yet, humility extends beyond self-awareness and respect. It also encompasses gratitude, the practice of acknowledging and appreciating the good in our life. It is about recognizing the contributions of others to our success, appreciating the opportunities we have been given, and expressing gratitude for our blessings. By embracing gratitude, we not only cultivate a sense of contentment and happiness but also strengthen our humility, thereby propelling us towards success.

However, humility is not about self-deprecation or lack of self-confidence. It is not about downplaying our achievements or undervaluing our worth. It is about maintaining a balanced view of ourselves, appreciating our worth without arrogance, and acknowledging our flaws without pretence. This balance between self-appreciation and self-criticism, between confidence and humility, is key to authentic humility.

In conclusion, the strength of humility is a powerful virtue, one that grounds our journey, enriches our relationships, and propels us towards success. By cultivating self-awareness, fostering respect, embracing gratitude, and maintaining a balance between self-appreciation and self-criticism, we can harness the strength of humility and steer our path towards success. As we journey through the chapters of this book, let us remember the wisdom of Jim Collins, "Greatness is not a function of circumstance. Greatness, it turns out, is largely a matter of conscious choice, and discipline." This is the strength of humility, the nineteenth step on our pathways to prosperity.

"The single biggest problem in communication is the illusion that it has taken place." - George Bernard Shaw

Chapter 20: The Essence of Communication

In the grand symphony of success and progress, communication serves as the melody. It is the harmonious tune that connects us to others, orchestrates our interactions, and ultimately, composes our life's music. It is the exchange of information, the sharing of thoughts, and the expression of feelings. This chapter, inspired by the wisdom encapsulated in "How to Win Friends and Influence People," explores the concept of communication and its pivotal role in our journey towards success and progress.

Communication, in its essence, is the practice of conveying information, expressing thoughts, and sharing feelings. It is about speaking with clarity, listening carefully, and responding with understanding. It is about connecting with others, building relationships, and fostering understanding. Above all, it is about recognizing the power of words and harnessing it to create a fulfilling and successful life.

At the heart of communication is the principle of clarity, the practice of expressing our thoughts, feelings, and ideas in a clear, concise, and coherent manner. It is about being precise in our speech, accurate in our descriptions, and consistent in our messages. By cultivating clarity, we not only enhance our communication but also foster a sense of understanding and coherence, thereby enriching our journey towards success.

Another key aspect of communication is empathy, seen as the practice of understanding and sharing the feelings of others. It is about listening with an open mind, responding with a compassionate heart, and connecting on an emotional level. By fostering empathy, we not only enhance our relationships but also deepen our communication, thereby empowering our journey towards success.

Communication, however, extends beyond clarity and empathy. Further, it encompasses respect, the practice of acknowledging and appreciating the thoughts, feelings, and perspectives of others. It is about valuing their opinions, respecting their experiences, and appreciating their contributions. By embracing respect, we not only cultivate a sense of dignity and worth but also strengthen our communication, thereby propelling us towards success.

Communication, however, must be separated from loquaciousness, dominating conversations or imposing our thoughts on others. It is about engaging in a mutual exchange of ideas, fostering a two-way dialogue, and creating a shared understanding. This balance between expressing ourselves and understanding others, between speaking and listening, is key to authentic communication.

In conclusion, communication is a powerful tool, one that connects us to others, enriches our relationships, and propels us towards success. By cultivating clarity, fostering empathy, embracing respect, and maintaining a balance between expression and understanding, we can master the essence of communication and steer our path towards success. As we journey through the chapters of this book, let us remember the wisdom of Dale Carnegie, "To be interesting, be interested." This is the essence of communication, the twentieth step on our pathways to prosperity.

"The capacity to learn is a gift; the ability to learn is a skill; the willingness to learn is a choice." - Brian Herbert

Chapter 21: The Journey of Lifelong Learning

In the grand voyage of success and progress, lifelong learning serves as the compass, the navigational tool that guides our exploration, directs our journey, and ultimately, charts our life's course. It is the continuous pursuit of knowledge, the ongoing quest for wisdom, and the perpetual journey of discovery. This chapter, inspired by the wisdom encapsulated in "Mindset: The New Psychology of Success," explores the concept of lifelong learning and its pivotal role in our journey towards success and progress.

Lifelong learning, in its essence, is the practice of continuous improvement, exploration, growing, and evolving. It is about seeking knowledge, pursuing wisdom, and exploring new horizons. It is about being curious, fostering creativity, and tasking the intellect. Above all, it is about recognizing the power of knowledge and harnessing it to create a fulfilling and successful life.

At the heart of lifelong learning is the principle of curiosity, the desire to discover, understand and master. It is about asking questions, seeking answers, and exploring possibilities. By cultivating curiosity, we not only enhance our learning but also foster a sense of wonder and fascination which are veritable tools to journey towards success.

A key ingredient to learning is openness, that is, the willingness to consider new ideas, perspectives, and paradigms. It is about challenging our assumptions, questioning our beliefs, and embracing change. By fostering openness, we not only enhance our adaptability but also deepen our learning, thereby empowering our journey towards success.

Yet, lifelong learning extends beyond curiosity and openness. It also encompasses persistence, the determination to keep learning, the resilience to overcome obstacles, and the grit to persist in the face of challenges. It is about persevering in our quest for knowledge, persisting in our pursuit of wisdom, and never giving up on our journey of learning. By embracing persistence, we not only cultivate a sense of determination and tenacity but also strengthen our lifelong learning, thereby propelling us towards success.

However, lifelong learning is not about hoarding knowledge or showcasing intellect. It is about applying our knowledge, sharing our wisdom, and using our intellect for the betterment of ourselves and others. This balance between learning and applying, between acquiring and sharing, is key to authentic lifelong learning.

In conclusion, the journey of lifelong learning is a powerful voyage, one that enriches our experiences, enhances our understanding, and propels us towards success. By cultivating curiosity, fostering openness, embracing persistence, and maintaining a balance between learning and applying, we can embark on the journey of lifelong learning and steer our path towards success. As we journey through the chapters of this book, let us remember the wisdom of Carol S. Dweck, "Becoming is better than being." This is the journey of lifelong learning, the twenty-first and final step on our pathways to prosperity.

"And, when you want something, all the universe conspires in helping you to achieve it." - Paulo Coelho, The Alchemist

Epilogue: The Symphony of Success

As we reach the end of this journey, let us pause for a moment and reflect on the wisdom we have gathered, the insights we have gleaned, and the lessons we have learned. This book, inspired by the profound wisdom of some of the greatest thought leaders and their seminal works, has been a voyage of discovery, a journey of exploration, and a quest for understanding.

We began with the power of vision and its pivotal role in guiding our path towards success. Then explored the importance of discipline, the strength of perseverance, the value of empathy, and the essence of communication. Further, we delved into the art of mindfulness, the influence of adaptability, and the journey of lifelong learning. Each chapter, each concept, and each insight assuredly added a unique note to our symphony of success, creating a harmonious melody that resonates with the rhythm of progress.

However, the wisdom encapsulated in this book is not an end in itself, but a means to an end. It is a compass to guide our journey, a map to chart our course, and a beacon to light our path. It is a tool to empower our growth, a resource to enrich our experiences, and a catalyst to propel our progress. It is not about achieving success in a day, a week, or a year, but about embarking on a lifelong journey of growth, progress, and fulfillment.

As we close this book, let us remember that the journey of success is not a sprint but a marathon, not a race but a voyage, not a destination but a journey. It is about embracing the journey with all its ups and downs, its twists and turns, its joys and sorrows. It is about cherishing each moment, savoring each experience, and celebrating each milestone.

In the grand symphony of success, each one of us is a unique note, a distinct melody, and a harmonious tune. Let us play our part with passion, perform our role with dedication, and contribute our share with enthusiasm. Let us create our own symphony of success, compose our own melody of progress, and orchestrate our own harmony of fulfillment.

As we embark on our unique journeys, let us remember the wisdom of Lao Tzu, "A journey of a thousand miles begins with a single step." Let us take that step with courage, continue that journey with perseverance, and complete that voyage with fulfillment. This is the symphony of success, the melody of progress, and the harmony of fulfillment. This is our journey, our voyage, our quest, our life. Let the journey continue...

REFERENCES

1. Covey, S. R. (1989). The 7 Habits of Highly Effective People: Powerful Lessons in Personal Change. Simon & Schuster.
2. Duhigg, C. (2012). The Power of Habit: Why We Do What We Do in Life and Business. Random House.
3. Tolle, E. (1997). The Power of Now: A Guide to Spiritual Enlightenment. New World Library.
4. Duckworth, A. (2016). Grit: The Power of Passion and Perseverance. Scribner.
5. Goleman, D. (1995). Emotional Intelligence. Bantam Books.
6. Collins, J. (2001). Good to Great: Why Some Companies Make the Leap... and Others Don't. HarperBusiness.
7. Dweck, C. S. (2006). Mindset: The New Psychology of Success. Random House.
8. Carnegie, D. (1936). How to Win Friends and Influence People. Simon & Schuster.
9. "Think and Grow Rich" - Napoleon Hill
10. "Who Moved My Cheese?" - Dr. Spencer Johnson
11. "Thinking, Fast and Slow" - Daniel Kahneman
12. "Success Through a Positive Mental Attitude" - Napoleon Hill and W. Clement Stone
13. "The Richest Man in Babylon" - George S. Clason
14. "Mindset: The New Psychology of Success" - Carol S. Dweck

15. "Tools of Titans: The Tactics, Routines, and Habits of Billionaires" - Timothy Ferriss
16. "The Role of Mindset in Personal and Organizational Success" - Carol S. Dweck, Psychological Science, 2006.
17. "The Science of Success: Understanding the Psychology of Achievement" - Angela Duckworth, Journal of Personality and Social Psychology, 2016.
18. "The Power of Now and the End of Suffering" - Eckhart Tolle, New Age Journal, 1997.
19. "The Role of Emotional Intelligence in Leadership" - Daniel Goleman, Leadership Quarterly, 1998.
20. "The Power of Habit: Why We Do What We Do in Life and Business" - Charles Duhigg, New York Times, 2012.
21. "The 7 Habits of Highly Effective People: Powerful Lessons in Personal Change" - Stephen R. Covey, Forbes, 1989.
22. "Good to Great: Why Some Companies Make the Leap... and Others Don't" - Jim Collins, Harvard Business Review, 2001.
23. "How to Win Friends and Influence People in the Digital Age" - Dale Carnegie, Time Magazine, 1936.
24. "The Role of Grit in Determining Success" - Angela Duckworth, Journal of Personality and Social Psychology, 2007.
25. "The Power of Positive Thinking: A Practical Guide to Mastering the Problems of Everyday Living" - Norman Vincent Peale, Positive Thinking Foundation, 1952.

www.ingramcontent.com/pod-product-compliance
Lightning Source LLC
Chambersburg PA
CBHW041522090426
42737CB00037B/3